where

stories

gather

where stories gather

POEMS

KARUNA EZARA PARIKH

HarperCollins *Publishers* India

First published in India by
HarperCollins *Publishers* in 2021
A-75, Sector 57, Noida, Uttar Pradesh 201301, India
www.harpercollins.co.in

2 4 6 8 10 9 7 5 3 1

P-ISBN: 978-93-5489-087-1
E-ISBN: 978-93-5489-095-6

Typeset in 11.5/15.5 Minion Pro at
Manipal Digital Systems, Manipal

Printed and bound at
Thomson Press (India) Ltd

FSC MIX Paper FSC® C010615

This book is produced from independently certified FSC® paper
to ensure responsible forest management.

For Omi
who crossed the oceans
to tell the first tale

Sometimes you are fire
burning with all your rage and might,
sometimes you're just like the moon
hanging lonely in the cold, cold night.
Sometimes you are stardust
swirling somewhere with the fireflies,
but always and forever,
it is you who are the light.

And for Arko
muse, keeper of my truth

All good men love the mountains
it's the rogues who love the sea,
I once met a man who loved both
and most of all he loved me.

Protector of travellers
Bless the road.

Watch over her in the desert
Watch over her in the mountain
Watch over her in the labyrinth.
Watch over her by the quicksand.

Protect her from the Voices.
Protect her from the Visions
Protect her in the tumult
Protect her in the silences.

[*They drink*]

– T.S. Eliot

Give me your darkness
and I'll give you mine
and like this, we'll create light.

Contents

Introduction

Though I only recently finished writing my first book, I can't recall the first poem I wrote. I must have been six or seven. And though I have been contemplating with awe the fact that I took my entire adult life so far to write a single novel, it struck me this morning that poetry has been with me for far longer. To put it simply – I have never known myself without poetry. It has been with me quietly my entire life.

As I'm sure it is with most poets, I spent many years filling notebooks with poems only for myself. When asked what I was writing, I would quickly draw the spiral-bound pages together, shutting secrets away. Then in my early teens, England's brilliant future poet laureate Benjamin Zephaniah visited my school. I got to spend a delicious afternoon listening to him do something I had never heard of called Spoken Word, and sharing with him my own poems. I recall experiencing the realization that one could *be a poet*. That it wasn't some sixteenth-century white male dream with quill and puffy sleeves. Inspired, I submitted a single poem to a national paper. It was called, rather ambitiously, 'Frigid Pulchritude'. I never heard back from them, and never again thought about publishing my work. Maybe my poetry was just for me or at the very most, for those I loved.

Then came the years of a twin awakening. On the one hand, at school I was learning about Plath and Donne and on the other, in my free time I was discovering the bounty of Bob Dylan and Jim Morrison and Jewel Kilcher. Of Cohen and Ginsberg and Patti Smith. Of Led Zep lyrics and 'a queen without a king' who 'plays guitar and cries and sings'. It is the truest thing for me to say: the intersection of rock n roll and literature is where I finally knelt and bowed my head to the glory of poetry.

In 2014, I was in Berlin for the summer under excruciatingly sad circumstances when I picked up a pen and jotted a poem onto a Post-it. On a whim, I uploaded it to social media using the hashtag #postitpoetryproject. I figured that by naming the thing I would be forced to write more for it. Life, as it does, got in the way. But abandoned by me as it later was, the idea did put me in the habit of writing poetry daily and in 2015, I wrote what my friends refer to as 'the Paris poem', using a slightly different format, and (being a child of the 'Millennia') a new hashtag: #prayfortheworld. The impact of that one poem, led to a certain degree of acceptance within me. Maybe I was *a poet*. The apprehension? I had never seriously studied or learnt poetry. Even now, like a child, I discover again and again that there are mighty, ancient systems in place which I haven't paid heed to. That there are Macaronic rhymes and Internal ones, Assonant and Consonant, Feminine and Masculine, Oblique and Perfect and Rich and Scarce. Knowing these exist fills me with awe and then quickly with regret and even sometimes shame. Where do *my* poems fall, I ask myself, panicked.

In an age when 'Instagram poets' are ubiquitous, and the discussion about their popularity and merit intermittently but consistently flares, it is terrifying to put out one's work. While it is an old fear for writers, that their words may not be well-received, or worse, misunderstood, the social media writer deals with a different and daily anxiety, counting self-worth out in 'likes' and 'followers', often confusing something as personal as poetry with something as fickle as popularity. From this space, it is even harder than usual to know the difference between what is truly good and what you are (consciously or not) putting out for instant gratification. What you have written to cleanse or challenge or give of yourself, and what you have unknowingly written to please others. What is – dare I say it – the heart's gimmick.

This is maybe why it has taken me so long to put out a book of poems. The truth is that in the wake of an available but shifty audience, I have been distrustful and therefore also disdainful of my own work, splattered across the internet. In the process, I have done it dishonor. Putting together *Where Stories Gather* has been a difficult task – sifting through years of work online and in notebooks, but also writing new poems, sometimes buoyant, sometimes heavy with the knowledge that they have the gravity of the published page ahead of them. Funny how something on the internet lasts 'forever' and every copy of a book can be destroyed, yet it is in the tangibility of the latter that we dock permanence. With this feeling I have torn into the writing, rebirthed it, immersed myself in the absolute privilege of creation and even then some days come up wondering if I am saying anything of value at all. But I have also been forced to ask, if only for the sake of steadfastness, if the profundity of a poem is diminished by say, its length? Or where it was first published. And if its impact is then diminished by a lack of profundity at all? If a single line has the power to move a single person, has its purpose been fulfilled? And if it affects someone, anyone, other than its own writer, by being expunged from that writer's twisted heart, is it valid then to publish it? Eventually there came the realization, that it is *only* the writing of it that matters. The rest, all of it, is simply grace granted.

Because poetry is so bare and honest a medium, reading one's own work is often like sitting with your family members. As with those other complicated relationships, you may not always like what you see. You cannot help but love it of course. Love is inexplicable. It comes from knowing fiercely what is ours and wanting to protect it. Like hate, it is beyond us. But *like*, is optional. And with poetry, the liking is as personal as with say a parent, a sibling, or a daughter. If I perceive shallowness there, it is because I know I have not gone deep enough. It leads one to admit: *I do not like this flaw in them, because it calls forth my own fault lines. But they are not less loved.* And ipso facto: *this may not be perfect, but I am not unloved.*

In my scribbled notes for this introduction it says: *Poetry has been the backbone of my life's experience. The knotted rope spine which I continue to climb*. I pondered this line and thought, yes, poetry has supported and even elevated me, but it is truer to say it has been my companion. From my father reciting whole passages of *The Rubaiyat of Omar Khayyam*, to my uncle doing Dylan Thomas better than Richard Burton. My mother's love for Rilke, my school principal stopping the morning assembly to read us 'Had I the Heavens …' or Tagore, my aunt introducing me to Maya Angelou, my college friends' devotion to Ghalib, my husband writing poems with me, line for line, in the early days of our courtship … poetry has tread softly all the corridors of my life. It is hard to remember a time before I didn't always have three things in my bag: a book, a journal and a pen. This has been their whispered song:

Listen, tell.
Absorb, expel.

And so, I found that reading and writing were the only things that calmed me or my need to bear witness. The thing that eased my heart, brought not just light but radiance to my darkest days, and showed me a path by which to continue on and process the sometimes seemingly impossible journey of life. The poems here, more than anything, are pieces of that processing. And if I am to finally answer for myself the question of what bears publishing, I must simply accept I have been inordinately moved time and time again, that these, my methods of processing resonate with others. Ironically, though my writing poetry was always a solitary act, often prompted by a feeling of immense isolation, sharing it is what helped me realize how very many of us there are in this together. I truly hope you enjoy the collection, and at the very least, that it serves as a reminder of this.

I

Become with every breath
that incredible thing
you so wish to be.

Admission

Tell me of your tidal dreams
and the anarchy budding
in the rich earth of your heart.
Tell me the rogue recipes
you have concocted quietly
in this time of sweet stillness
and the tune of the slow jazz
you have danced to alone
in your living room
that has had no visitors
in months.
Tell me of all the plans you
held fast to your chest then
crumpled up as the future fell away
and tell me how you later took your list
back from the bin, pressed out its creases
and refolded it into origami discernible
to and unfoldable by only you.
Tell me of your meditations on solitude
and how it is this coarse thing
we are only just befriending.
Tell me all of how you breathed life
into a world you did not recognize
but made human, the only way you knew how.
Tell me,
and I will tell you all mine.

Confession

I stress scratch
break hapless skin
pick at unready scabs then blot blood
watch party nail polish grow out.
Putting my words out here
on the permanence and transience
of the page, blazing honest, dirty
feels like the dream
when you leave the house naked
all your foolish parts on display
belly and blossoming hair,
crumply knees, grey like elbow
like neglect.
Who are these folk with smooth corners
and do they ever write poems?
About choking fear and what it feels like
to feel ugly?
My fingers are grubby at best.
The soles of my feet
have gnawed this bad world
and their cracked edges
like pig teeth, chew earth.
I am humus,
but I am planting in my
seeming decay
rich futures.

Gathering

Imagine going back
to before the first panic attack
before the world revealed itself
as the flimsy neon-edged thing it is
and your teeth were intact, once
you had never woken to the dust
of your own enamel in your own mauve mouth
that place supposedly full of kisses
waiting to be given as reward
for winning your brittle, fickle heart.
Once you were not something to unknot
you were whole as Solan pickled plums
once you were unbred by politics
cusping on curiosity not spent
on the daily pounding of persistent anger
imagine if you knew no thieving of breath
no shame of tears in the sticky velour back of a taxi cab
as you wail *I don't know I don't know I don't know*
and the one person you trust says *it's okay it's okay it's okay*,
on that untrustworthy machine, your phone,
but it isn't [okay], but hush, hush, imagine,
before all this somewhere
you were being born
you were a prawn-head, crinkle-butt, flush-face,
you were a speck you were atoms gathering,
weightless space then not
once, you were a moment of want.

Growing Up on a Farm Called Stonehenge

When I am 14 we move to a farm.
The internet has arrived everywhere
but for us. I am unable to add to the
school exchange of conversations
swivelling around Pamela Anderson,
Beverly Hills and bold beautiful things.
Cable TV is something extraordinary
but not for me. Mercifully there are CDs.
At night I play, in my humungous
hollow cave of a room on repeat
four white boys screaming about
Immigrants and Heaven and Kashmir.
There is deep solace in rock 'n' roll.
My boyfriend takes the bus – 519
to the end of the line – to see me.
We joke about the goats on the road.
When we arrive my sisters and I late
each week to school maybe three of five days
and say the cattle were crossing again
there is disbelief or quite likely it is disdain.
Town mice and country mice cross paths again.
I remember the confusion of hearing of
these mice. Thinking – isn't a country bigger?
Learning the difference between *a* and *the* –
or was there any? Unsure.
Because my teenage hands have pulled potatoes and

planted papaya trees. Beloved guava, anaar, broccoli.
The first cow came she was called Licorice
dark as night and angry maybe because I drank so much
of her milk meant for her baby Fruit Salad the one with a
star between her eyes she was
the first born child at Stonehenge
like hope or revenge for all that would later die.
Lizards exponentiated and one winter the owls arrive
two fistfuls of silent fluff necks just spinning tufts and
expanding eyes they are what everyone stayed for.
And the fireplace that is no more.
The lights were always dim, slow to start, and we sleep
five to a room in a house for a hundred, maybe scared of
drifting for too long too far apart.
Wait, I must go back to the fireplace.
The tiles – blue and white Iznik like the Ottomans used –
came from Turkey – oh the colossal luxury of it all! Anatolia –
just the word made people ooh and aah while drinking
my dad's velvet wines in the rose garden behind the pool
empty because my mother couldn't bear to waste water.
There are good moments by the fireplace. Mostly there is
pain. Crowds come for parties unwitness to the sadness
the stone walls hold in, presenting as perfect for guests.
But we know where the ghosts live.
We don't go near the compost pit or sewage tanks
filled with all our shit, smelling rank a reminder

that even here with all our seed and bee theories
we damage everything we touch. Even so
there is a tree down where the caretaker stays.
Six soft small palms have climbed it, made grooves
with small bums in the places bark meets bark, cheaply
I always took the best seat and we coloured in things
and even the tree (I think she's a neem) will say it was okay.
It was alright that we wiggled tiny toes into root and made
whole branches our own, dogs at the foot, waiting.
It's okay because there was a dog in every bed, sometimes
three or five or eight, sometimes if we are lucky a snake.
How quickly my tenses, flippant as memory, change from
past to present and back again – no writing flaw this –
I am in all the places at once. In the silence before and
after the world ended and the world continued and the
ghost piano played my mother's tunes on its own.
One winter when everything is almost forgotten,
my dad comes in like a whirlwind with the neighbour's
Chinese oranges. I didn't know we had neighbours but
here is proof – small succulent bittersweet mounds.
He rolls his business shirtsleeves up, gets his thick hands
to work and dirty and turns the long kitchen into
Christmas, making marmalade cauldron upon cauldron
and casts with simple sugar grains a spell of happiness.
Like this I learn to bring back time. Living with ghosts is

easier for me than living with nothing, though you're free to
disagree. So I barbeque. Ask for khurpi to check kyaaris
for iceberg lettuce and gobi. As always there's too much
mooli and dhania, always dhania. My room stays
ready to receive. The dogs sleep. Like this past is present
and back again. I still don't know how to switch on a television.

Submission

The ancient
city of your heart
is big and beautiful
and intricate and vast.
Do not surrender it so easily.
Your ramparts are the thickest
most marvelous edge to a world
I have ever seen. Just behind the lip
lies a country of Calvino capitals, of
pink spiral stairways and molded ceilings
where the lost sparrows of Delhi craft nests
in corners and in cascades of bougainvillea
bough the shade of your lipstick and tongue
like a drawbridge. Keep it up, keep unbesieged
this palace of dreams. Keep the drums thrumming
and bless your firelight as night knits with dark hands
a cloud to pull over you to keep your bounties safe that
you may create symmetries of self-promise, of tomorrows
with roots in the trellis of yesterday's widespread wisdoms.
You hold in your stony bosom enough bedtime stories
for ten generations of subjects to worship.
Surrender? *No.* Raise your sword.
Who bows low might be granted
a crack in your door.

Becoming

You are not the sum of the people you have loved.
You are not the sum of the ones you have tried to,
nor the ones you didn't but left your mark upon anyway.
Even in your wakeful, difficult, sizzling cruelty,
you are math more dignified than that.

You are not your favourite grey T-shirt or your
even now unquenched thirst for single malt.
You aren't your first-grade teacher's prophecy
from when you were filled with an abundance of hope,
nor are you your ninth-grade teacher's warning,
from when you began to lose in bundles, the same.

But maybe you are your big smile. At least
that is how I would like to think of you. Your massive
heart might as well be secretly filled with forest flowers
coming up as merry pranksters in its mulchy groves.

And maybe, at least for me,
you are the sunrise splashed across the sky.
So brave in your bloodiness, forever rising even after sinking.
Fearlessly warm, transforming everything in your fiery wake.

Maybe, in the years no one was watching,
you unwrapped your litany of wounds,
drew time out like a ribbon to yourself,
and maybe just maybe, like a gift,
you became hope itself.

Home

It took me a long time
to come into my own,
but now that I'm here
I plan to inhabit me completely.

I plan to eat all the lotuses
turn myself into royalty
learn to cartwheel so that
I may conquer the world
and all its islands upside down.

I plan to watch seven hundred
and thirty sunrises and sets.

Dine on rosebuds and
in place of long legs grow a tail
swish sadness away
like a swallow or mermaid
or some wild winged thing,
and I will float as opposed to walk,
illegal as it may be.

Come!

I plan to feel the earth in my bones,
tend difficult Gondhoraj till it thrives
at the swinging altar of my knees,
comb my hair with shark fishbone,
and drink honey straight from
the mouths of bees.

It's time. *I'm ready.*

Bone Work

Do the bone work.
Ask yourself –
What am I feeling?
Will this break me or is that creak
just the sound of my skeleton
stretching to make room
for my soul's swelling?

II

Spider lick on breast –
she is a seamstress mending.
She knows what is torn.

Let us talk more now of women with unafraid mouths.

Who speak
and kiss
and eat
fearlessly.

Ravenous.

Women whose dark mouths sing songs in the key of brave.

Who have spat out shame.

Whose every smile is glory.
Every laugh a revolution.

Let us talk with more love of women who might bite

and why.

Waiting at the Gynaecologist's Office

The nervous ticks of women repulse me and too
often involve nails. One clicks two together, flicking
them infuriatingly. If I close my eyes I can pretend
they are knitting needles – a thing of creation then, not
an ordeal. Another one talking in vitro, taps false ones
tik tik tik on the steel chair we share, it has been hours
I wish they'd break but she doesn't pay that much
for nothing. She knows the magic of science. A tall girl
opposite is using one to scrape dirt from beneath another. One
gnaws hers down to their calcic bone. Raw-cuticled she holds
tests to her enormous belly and small chest. I look away.
Old lady with blood stains and a balloon that says Get Well Soon.
There is someone tearing split-ends from single strands of hair.
It's better than ball scratching but still I am unkind. Sniff,
switch seats away from the baby so blessedly soft I could kill
it with a squeeze – how do people, I mean we, bear them?
Many come with men – the worst habit of all – and the lords
belch and bob stomachs into the backs of women in line,
sickeningly proud of what their sperm has done. How it
has made them useful after all. They usher, the tired shoulders
of their wives have never felt so gallanted. My fitness feels
barren. There are smells that bring to mind the word 'streak'.
I push away wave upon wave of nausea, of the tremor of musky
trepidation that comes each time you are made to lay
on your back with your pants down and your legs wide,
your cunt up, to her mistress the moon, but not for love.

I have grown up angry
I cannot walk the streets
wearing what I please
living in a country
made of heat –
none of which
can belong to me.*

(*When all of it belongs to me.)

Sample Collection

Tell me the real statistics.
Tell me how many men are doing the raping.

Where Stories Gather

When we stop forgiving
in our fathers
/ uncles
/ brothers
/ lovers
/ friends
/ sons
what we have held against
the other ones.

(that time someone passing by on a bike stroked your proud bare summer calf in the rickshaw, cutting your laughter to gasp and you told the sweet boy by you and he said 'are you sure' and you were suddenly not sure / that uncle / that tuitions master under the dining table with the same hand he drank chai in your ma's china and there were biscuit crumbs inside you later [it was how you discovered you had an inside] / that date [you had said 'I'd rather not' and later you said in your head fuck it ab kya] later you could not understand if it warranted a 'me too' status or not / you still don't know so it's best not to / you stay up late wondering if your silence affects statistics / if you are a statistic / that sweet cook who sent your niece photos of dogs fucking, you remember? She was a feisty one she had said 'he calls me sometimes at night' she was 12 everyone told her to shut up with her stories / it reminded you of that time you were 3 and you thought his wetness on your hand was your fault / maybe this is how we became storytellers)

The Great Indian Rope Trick

There is a woman in me rising
out of all the ones that aren't.

She is being pulled forth
by the oiled plait of her dark hair
slithering skyward –
will it turn to noose
halfway, like a trick?
Is it even a sky or a blue glass
ceiling waiting sharp, a vicious
cloud festooned guillotine.

She is being born, lotus-foot-first,
running, baby bud feet on cracked earth,
she is surpassing six million years
of something erroneously called evolution,
a pataki, an umbilical cord shooting backwards
through time, to chase down the first patriarch
and feed him the tough seeds of his daughter's freedom.

She is rising and rising through the fault lines
of failed humanity, bursting,

like some manic radical stalk
through history
to seize and scoop through the soil
all the ones that aren't
till they come gasping up for the air
that's forever been theirs.

Stone

Do not give me diamonds,
for my heart is the biggest one of all.
See how hard it is to cut,
see how it glitters even as you seek its flaws.

Sass

I am a feminist
in love (with a man).
Believe me, there is no fiercer thing.
I am here to prove I can love and be loved
equally. I am here to claim what I deserve.

Amendments

Spending great time these days
praying for the future redundance
of all these poems about women and womanhood
and happy sappy women's day
because what is ~~gender~~?

He wants to wear skirts this boy,
something about that makes me want to
just kiss him cheek to cheek, lounging together
in floral maxis raucous painted rum drunk aunties,
maybe him and me and a matching plastic plate
of pakore because he wants to share lipsticks, why,
I was married in a suit. I was bald by choice.

What are these tense lines drawn so tight between
his him and my her –
they hurt and
who said heels are for me
and me of breast or vagina only?
His calves look so frickin' fine in them
curls of hair unfurling broadly off
his flexed muscles that resemble god
as he walks his very straight
very cis very sweet Miss
of a girlfriend home in her
shocking clothes – jeans.

Navigation

If I post naked pictures will you like me more
will it be easier to hate me
will you sit and count flaws will you
call me slut but follow me anyway
lusting after my photoshop
if I post photos where I look thin and
stare glassy eyed out of frame
and caption them 'dreaming of pizza
of thali of golgappa of burger of cake'
will you double tap that shit
because my lie might make you feel bad about yourself
but somehow that self loathing
I could unknowingly trigger in you
would keep you coming back for more.
When people double tap that shit
do they realize they're buying into photoshop lies
that their likes eventually make the photographed
feel just as bad, or so much worse for wear –
how does one show truth now?
If I post my skin as app-perfect
will I be worthy of blue ticks?
If I reveal underboob but not nipple
am I handing out just the right amount of excitement

you know, before it turns to discomfort
before it can be reported.
If I show crotch but never mention it bleeding
am I whole? Pure?
If I wrote poems on my ass
would you read them then?

Selfish

I eat vitamins that I am told
will make my body a good host
for seed to hug sperm and win
the synchronized swimming Olympics
hosted by the ancient city of my body
this year (next will be too late for the event).
I look at children, find them furless
things to cuddle, shrill, frail, ungrateful things,
unhappy to have life thrust upon them by you.
I think how brave to keep expunging them
from womb as the world begins to end.
When the world ends I wonder quietly
would you leave them behind?
I cannot comprehend how and when
I grew so selfish.
One night I see a picture
of a pair of boots the size of my palm,
something throbs, I think
this is not an ache, but
I can't place it,
what did I eat?
Until I accept it is womb growl,
all but a prune now
thirty seven, that's old to start

taking vitamins as hope.
I stand sideways in the mirror
and think it could be cute,
I could raise her like a
rare, furless, baby wolf.
Maybe I just always liked boots.

Survival

I have an unrivalled capacity
for self-destruction,
but that being said,
I can draw the Phoenix
from absolutely any fatality.

Waiting

Gentle
is just fierce
resting.

III

The moment in the
healing when you see they were
always unworthy.

Q) Why do you travel constantly?

A) So that sadness doesn't find me.

Reflection

(2017)

I know you're sad
but don't be.
It's not so good for your face.

Also, I've noticed your appetite suffers,
and I never did like 'thin' very much.
Neither did you.
We both preferred robustness –
strong shoulders, lofty chests,
feet so firm they could swirl about leaving stories
like plump strokes of a paintbrush.

In the same way we both liked mountains.

I know it hurts
but try and be a mountain.
They've seen everything,
but imagine what they'd be
if they had allowed it to make them sad.
Imagine, if they had allowed it to bring them down.

(2021)

I was wrong maybe.
Mountains are essentially
devastated beings.
All those rivulets of saltless water
streaming down aged crevasses
of mineral skin grown thick from sorrow.
Mountains have always been the
oldest sadness on Earth.
Rising up to contain all
our collective mortality
while still seeking stars.
An entire doomed planet's
first and last gravestones.
Look at the lands the Himalayas
must witness each day. See
how they rose to contain our pain.
They say the Alps expanded
many significant inches
during World War Two.
If you don't believe me,
talk to the Afghans.
I know it hurts.
Go give it to the mountains.

Mourning

Tonight, take time to remember
then tomorrow forget.
Healing is just the process
of letting go of regret.

Fated

I miss your palm on my breast.
Not because like heat it brought back to life my skin,
or because of what had just passed between us.
Nor because you followed it
with a comment on my supposed perfection
which you, like lovers do,
thought was innate.
But because in those moments
I could swear
your lifeline and mine
had conversation
and made such thick promises
to one another,
that flesh retreated,
humbled,
and simply gave up
vying for attention.

All wounds must worsen before they close,
remember the person and not what they chose.
All wounds must worsen before they close,
remember the person and not what they chose.
All wounds must worsen before they close,
remember the person and not what they chose.
All wounds must worsen before they close,
remember the person and not what they chose.
All wounds must worsen before they close,
remember the person and not what they chose.
All wounds must worsen before they close,
remember the person and not what they chose.
All wounds must worsen before they close,
remember the person and not what they chose.
All wounds must worsen before they close,
remember the person and not what they chose.
All wounds must worsen before they close,
remember the person and not what they chose.
All wounds must worsen before they close,
remember the person and not what they chose.
All wounds must worsen before they close,
remember the person and not what they chose.
All wounds must worsen before they close,
remember the person and not what they chose.

In the Days of Separate Lives

And so I learnt how to live without your laughter,
because it meant I could live without always being late.
I learnt to put on a nice dress and comb my hair
even if I was alone,
because if a tree falls in the forest
and there is no one there to hear it
a tree has still fallen in the forest.
I learnt to grow so large I could fill a bed
which earlier you and I and all our dogs
and every one of our sadnesses never could.
I learnt that one single person rising all alone
can grow to fill what two people falling out of love
together could never.
We used to lie on opposite ends
three feet of bedsheet
an impossible ice desert to cross.
We used to lie entwined like ghosts.
I have now learnt the solitude
of lying in my own arms.
I have learnt to be firm,
to repaint the edges of my body
that had disappeared like vapour in search of stars.
Today I am so vast I turn whole rooms into my own.
Sometimes at night I wake scared and small.
I take a sip of cold water and expand again.
I am a giant and I am filled with nothing but my own love.

Over

i

There were things we never said
and words that were never spoken
because long before we parted ways
our hearts were already broken.

ii

Now gently we move to forgetting
like corn stalks flossing the summer air
tossing the blonde tips of their hair
like girls who have lost everything
but still choose to dance
to the thrum of bees
hoping for one
rum tongued fumble
that might set them free.

Space Poems

i

When I began to fall in love with you
little by little
my feet stopped touching the ground.
Maybe because most of the time
my long legs were locked
behind your strong back.
Other times
I'd simply swim
from room to room
like an astronaut
fevered as a dervish.
These days
in your absence
I am discovering the Earth
like we once discovered comets.
I plant difficult dreams,
I wait for them to grow.
Someday maybe they will grow so tall
I'll climb up them
to that place we once lived.
To where gravity did not exist.

ii

Keep some kisses secret
in the inside of your thigh.
In that place of softness
where gravity does not exist.
Take them out when you need to
and replace those blank spaces
to the side of your tongue.
Like this, remember me
in the days to come
when we are apart.

Ill Fated

Remember when I said your hands were tender as new roses?
I said, 'Give them to me, since you never give me flowers.'
You brought them together to make a bouquet
or maybe just to pray
that this would work.
I pulled them to my mouth
to taste what was true.
As I kissed each fine finger
like plucking petals,
I counted in hope –
You love me
you love me not.
But ten is not a lucky number.

Call me,
if you are ever this side
of the universe my friend

no matter how many lifetimes
have passed by then

I would like to someday dissect
the anatomy of kisses again.

A Personal Manual to Make a Heart Stop Hurting

Every single thing you wish they could do,
you begin to do for you.
So you wake up tomorrow – begin just there –
and make yourself tea.
Flavour it with mint or rose petals or cardamom or ginger –
whatever you like most.
Then drink it listening to Billie Holiday,
Dusty Springfield, Hari Prasad Chaurasia
or anyone else who makes your bones come alive.
The genius of your standing skeleton is that it can dance.
Bathe.
Water is the refuge of the broken-hearted
because crying in the ocean is just replenishing it.
Cry in the shower –
it is the second most graceful place to do that.
Wear the green pantsuit you reserved for them,
when you reserved a table at that new Burmese restaurant
you thought they would like to try.
Put on your red lipstick. Or don't ever again.
Also don't bother with heels if you don't want to.
(Much as you may repeat it to colleagues,
your life is not a balancing act.)
Work.
Work so hard your castle descends from the air for you

brick by sturdy sacred brick.
And when your day is done,
stop by the flower shop
and buy yourself some tulips.
Bring them home and place them in the tall glass vase
that lies empty too often.
Lay down.
Stretch.
Now book a ticket
to that place you thought
you would go together.
Pour a glass of wine.
This is your life
you're going to be fine.

Folk Song I

You who taught me the taste of tears,
must be reminded in your regret,
of the story of the king with three daughters.

On asking which one loved him the most,
one said he was like silver,
the other compared him to gold.
The third, the youngest, said without a doubt,
she cherished him as much as salt.

And so his anger came to this,
he chose her to be dismissed.
That night the cooks prepared a feast,
they upturned soil and roasted beast.
But when the king sat down to eat,
he found the meal was incomplete.

After hullaballoo and huge uproar,
the king fell weeping on the floor.
'Call the princess home,' he said,
'and hand her the keys to the kingdom instead.'

And this was how it came to pass,
that salt like love, is given not asked.
And let this be the final lesson,
that salt in any form, is blessing.

If you cease to love me
do not worry.
I will slip away
in the dead of night,
so silent
you will not be able to count my footsteps.
In fact, you will not even know I was ever there
save the scent of powder on your pillow.
I will disappear so deeply
even the vast scape of your memories
will not be able to resurrect me.

Someday, years from now,
We will cross paths perhaps
in a café in a side street
in a cobblestoned piazza of yore.
Or a cold airport lounge at dawn.
You will pause over paying for coffee and think,
'Now that's a face I could fall in love with!'
And I will smile
and never let you know
that once upon a time,
you did.

IV

Of all the things our love
could have been, unrequited
was never one of them.

For you I will set up home on a ship,
the back of an elephant,
an attic, a palace,
a shoebox,
a matchbox,
a mansion
a tulip
a shell.

(For you I will do the impossible thing,
for you I will start again.)

Monsoon I

Just before it rains my scars begin to ache
the same way it aches between my thighs
every time we are meant to meet.
In anticipation of wetness
in want of release
in unending hope
these wounds
will be healed.

Unbound

You say you need to gather yourself.
I want to tell you I will gather you instead.
I will collect your stranded pieces living
like islands apart, in my downy green arms,
smudge out those rough-hewn edges
scratched by burr, that chafe and churn.
You were never told they were a world but
I'll call cloud to the hot sun hurt of your spider-bit heart
and make blossom your happiness like twice-fed roses.
I will feed you honeywine from my hands
and restore the skin
you are trying to fertilize with tears.
We will dance the dance of the unbroken
around the fire then
we will unbind the constellations
star by bloody star.

Breaking Bread

How to measure sadness?

In thimbles of tears?

In white scars up a wrist
climbing the ladder of this
skinny brown arm
slender rungs
of sorrow.

Perhaps there exists somewhere
a weighing scale for the heart
to determine how much heavier it is
from one day to the next.

Perhaps it is truth –
an empty heart is *not* less heavy.

But
in the midst of life's grieving,
behold,
there are days cotton lined,
washed silver with wine
in the scalloped chatter
of friends beneath blankets
like small turtles

necks crooked
staring sleepily out toward Galaxy –
is this the first, prehistoric gesture of faith?
To become curled thumbs, backs against the earth,
open to yet safe from alien invasion, together.

Behold
in the creamy recollection of sharp notes
we have sung in sync before,
crisp guitars call, heavy tongues walk into song.
There is nonsense language we have made up over the years,
and we speak it now, words warm as bonfire.

The hand on the heart-scale does not move.
It sits, palm to chest, the thimble runs dry,
and the scars turn inward, invisible,
who needs ladders when you are flying.

Peaches, Not Canned

Your soul is made of laughter.

Replenish.

Pour it down your spirit's throat
till you want to spit it out again,
then let the giggles come forth –
pink and bubbly, fizzing from the body,
a bottle of perpetually spilling champagne.
This giddiness a lighthouse bearing your name.

Wash away that known swampy grief
with soft, light, curls of mirth –
they made me fall so
mightily in love,
took me by the wrist,
into your summer home bits,
your place of promised happiness
of fresh peaches just torn and ready.

In that place of ever-light,
hear me say –
Laugh. Laugh again.
Replenish you.
Oh help me,
replenish me.

Show Me

Show me the hardest part of you
and I will be soft with it.
Then show me where you are softest...
and I will be softer still.

V

Some days I break down
But some days, I break even.
(Balancing my books.)

I am
easily hurt
everything feels like
codswallop
my heart is a marshmallow
melting behind the bonfire heat
of my resting bitch face.
I am constantly cut
by the shards of my own
silly sharp-angled soul
after it has raised
its hair to splinter
like a dog, scared.

Here

I love your accent
where is it *from?*
Is one more way
of trying to gauge
where on a map to place
my sweet shade of skin.
The question of from
always presents as a puzzle.
From seed, from divine,
from monkeys walking –
me and trees share DNA!
I want to remind you my body is water.
I have heard too often how our skin
is made from battered old stars.
My grandmother who prefers
lavender both in scent and shade
knows all the tree names
linden-soaped white skin she
grew up on a farm in Germany.
She talks of the big war
and when the planes tossing bombs came.
She met a forever-man from Bengal
but you ask where am I from?
Together they drew the latitudes together.
Perhaps my accent is an aural topography of their love.
Can you find in the geography of my mixed body
their failed efforts at silencing your question?

2002

Cold Cardiff that knew no summer
six girls in a shared gingerbread house
the kitchen a conference in egg diplomacy,
closets bursting with denim and spandex,
the calendar a countdown of ova.

One night I need wine –
The Lebanese is coming over, with sushi.
(I have never consumed raw fish
or a Lebanese before.)
Five frantic voices shriek 'Go! Just go!'

White cotton lace-frilled nightie from Calcutta
straps so delicate they could snap if
my laughter rises an octave, if my nipples decide to sing.
I pull my maroon coat over my bare brown arms but no bra,
I leave barefoot for Tesco.

'Look at the little Indian go!' they cheer, thrilled and
appalled by this imagined savage correctness. I run my
gleeful heart racing my bare feet and I am not offended,
I am beloved. Is this context, is this ignorance, is this
self-loathing or their not knowing or mine?

Worthy

Self care always shown as bubble baths
aromatherapy (where you smell good things)
and pedicures on pearly toed feet.
The first time I entered a salon they asked me
if I don't bleach – just like that in the negative
to imply in any case of doubt, to not was wrong.
You don't bleach?
Where, I asked in bafflement.
(Tell me, I want to be beautiful too.)
Your face
back
thighs
arms
ass
breasts are too tan
but how?
My desi chest has never even once met the sun!

I stare at the slippery beauty magazine in my lap
as they chit chat and cut the dyed blonde hair
of a milky kudi who is offered green tea as
I sit thirsty my scabby knees peeking from under
a summer dress I believed made me pretty but

now I tense sweat, thighs sticking to seat, I shift
and notice they are patchy and look like filth.

My first experience in self care was
a lesson in fighting shame. Assuring my young body
it was vastly deserving of more than just pedicures.

Warning

Just because my skin is the colour of earth
just because my eyes are the dark stones of your dreams
just because flowers erupt from me in cascades
my hair resembles root
moons bloom in the heat of my very presence
and I can weep a river that tastes of the sea.
Just because my skin is the colour of earth
does not mean you may plant
your sorrows
your seed
your hell of false ideals
your weak anger
in me.

Heroine

I repeat, I like

skin

like earth.

The shade of dirt.

Craters
calling homage to the past,
here lava has licked the
epidermis where time
has not stood still,
where stories gather
not as fault lines but as river beds
thick with silt and fish egg,
and all of life's debris.
Cheeks carved with the laughing memory
of underwear slipped from summer thighs,
rippling and dimpled gloriously by
bunchfuls of golden old romps.

Imagine the skin of a life
with every adventure taken.
A pulse pushed up always
right against it, so close to the edge

any moment now flesh might fail, may
trip, break, burst and show blood, could
betray this body as human. But till then
let the beat match a butterfly and
maybe you'll understand when I say –

I like skin

you can count

constellations in. Like:

there look, the story of a hero,
oh there look, another one!

Loser

Teenager, legs like toothpicks
sagging knees and frumpy skirt still too short to cover them.
I took everything bad out on my hair (purple shaved mess)
and everything good out on my bedroom walls (first poems).
I remember being tufty in several ways, even in my soul,
and too brown, too angular, too graceless (god, having
too many silver square braces) to win.
I wasn't original in my pain
despite feeling I had more of it
than other people, and channelling it loudly into tattoos
building my own lore, and listening to The Doors
like everyone else.
I thought maybe I was the only one dancing with fire
drinking from skulls, drinking endlessly,
how funny, these are human phases, they pass.
As adults we laugh about it over Chenin Blancs
exchange traumas like we once did stickers and slam books
and early STDs, and say 'you too? (exclamation exclamation)'.
I leave cocktail parties learning I was typical
so tell me (I'm screaming this part now)
why did I feel so alone?
No child should think
being disastrous is maybe
what makes you special.
It's been almost twenty years

since I left school, and
I'm still asking
if maybe it does.
Tell me, how do I learn to be
anything better than twisted
and tell me
would I still catch your eye
if I were.

The Privilege

I have been reckless with my girls
flimsy as chiffon skirts we have behaved
irreverent as petals falling, flipping up in the wind.

One, she was a sprite made of jazz and muscle but
even small men could capsize her with say
a cigarette, a poem, a punch in the face.

The other she was short, bum like
a temple dancer, decidedly atheist
pocket full of pot, a knife tongue of a girl, but still.

Soft as three gummi bears we would ride
through the Rape Capital of the World
drunk on freedom, taking lusty long man-less sips of it.

Cheap whiskey breath, stockinged legs I have
mostly lived immortal, but one night we are caught in fog.
Nature's unexpected treachery binds us closer.

We go silent, peering, fear grips us by the vulva and
heat fizzes quickly out of scotch-bred throats as
a truck-beast looms up on a road name we don't know.

We are frozen as ice cubes, till one of us decides to
roll down her window, lean out against headlight,
a loon facing doom, scooped crimson winter cloak
revealing neck, arched for death.

She says breathlessly, 'Bhaiyya maachis hai?'
Everything pauses. He tosses down the box like fire from his loins,
at her, like he won. She lights up, a brown lock blows sex.
An ember guides us home.

Later I sleep between them, fuzzy as bunnies. I ask myself –
what saved us? Her beauty, the other one's caste, the accent,
the big white car? I tuck guilt beneath the pillow
for every night I dream instead of die.

Nobody Knows

To ditch that deepest and shallowest fear
of not being good enough.
That somewhere there is a secret party,
a clustering of all the perfect people you envy
(and it is envy you feel, why dress it up as you do
as hate and disdain and even sordidly – hurt)
talking over hard cocktails
(they can hold their liquor)
the silver not the colourful kind
(they're grown-ups unlike you)
with firm olives, from the countries whose politics
and poetry they know backwards, could recite
melodious in their safe, unclenched sleep.
They are discussing how ridiculous you are and
how your art has no meaning.
But look – even here, in dread (or is it dream?)
you have made yourself too important
when even now,
the work is waiting.

VI

...the funny thing is,
the more walls I brought down, the
safer I became.

How Do Poets Write

How do poets write only of important things?
Could I? Of men touching me with
hands of sawdust and grease
you know the feeling;
of Syria, Lebanon, groves of blood and olives,
magenta streeted towns emptied of bodies
(and the bodies left are empty)
erupted architecture and
mourned empires soon to be forgotten.
I have banished the thought of their pets.
Shall I write of disease and all those
incurable things that one half of the world
believes could never happen to them.
What does one say about the ripe fanatics
surrounding us, so close now
we could even tango, we could
stick our tongues out and lick
the poison off the hairy ears of these
folk who wield their crafty tool tyranny.
Shall I waste ink on the zombie electorate
corpus of hate, serving the company of
outliers to the olden systems of love.
How men with beards are more likely
to disappear here even as these mega prized cities
slip violently to sea, a little more each year.
Let me write of the thing that stays
let me write of the unimportant moon.

Monsoon II

And still the rain will come
still the sky will darken
like your mood these days
still the afternoon will bring
choppy breeze across the tops of city trees
and wily blood drawing winged creatures
in somehow through your netted window
and still the leaders will not lead
us anywhere but to a place worse
and still we will catch sadness and disease
but still, here see, monsoon will come
we will accept the half sun for months,
we will ignore half moons
and half truths, celebrate halfwits
and still, we will use the word democracy
as the rivers dry and then fill again
and still we will forget that
there are some things unlike seasons
that we can choose
that we can elect
yet still.

Hearing Jan Gan Man Precisely Mid-August

Coming in on the end of Shravan.
Somewhere in the close distance
across the almost autumn park
I hear *jaya hai jaya hai*
my heart stands up I try to swallow it
but it is so swollen with sudden identity.
I feel cheap like aching for a lover
because of Julia Roberts.
I may as well brandish a satin tiranga
and call it silk.
Aren't I better than a patriot
aren't I more than a heartstring pulled
ferociously by song
by fucking *anthem*?
I am collapsing against myself
and the hard memory
handed down ancestrally
blood to blood so to speak
of battles fought *of country uncut*
of freedom and trysts with what was meant to be ours.
When were we last proud in the now
without anthem or flag bringing
pride then downfall?

Bringing forth sorrow like a wound
like the parting of earth like skin.

Before, in a village in Gujarat
my grandfather's neighbour used to call out to him
offering biryani (with saffron and succulent meat) each Eid.
I talk to the dead, ask this strict vegetarian ancestor –
Dada, how did you eat it?
He laughs, won't tell me.
Instead he tells me how they played cricket
between unpartitioned courtyards
him and his neighbour, Akber Ali.
Technically, he is still our neighbour
he says in a dream.
Today both sides say –
The ball's in your court.
Confusing stuff in a game of Bluff.

Write About What Hurts

Let us write of anything but the Jamun trees. Anything but
the speaking network of root and how squirrels have nested
in its breast tendering for a hundred years their stripes
upon furred sure-footed children. Let us not speak now
of the letter, once handwritten and kept, informing
of Mangal Pandey's death or access that memory
of a boy you once loved, taking your dove hand to his
on the damp grass where grown men lithely blew rainbowed
soap bubbles as slippery and fast disappearing as our oil.
What of the time you held the idea of nation dear, suddenly
a cricket fan, suddenly waving a flag under the stout arch
of India Gate because in victory we all want to belong.
Remember your 31st birthday, Madras checked sari, you were
a step from discovery that year and when asked you said
take me there to the very throat of the city, that crosspoint
where oxygen enters its lungs, vitally, where taste becomes
sustenance. Let's talk of anything but the arts and the five
stones that were brought from five rivers to inaugurate again
our deep love for them. What of the five trees or the sleeping
Deodar? No, let us not because there were seven cities, like
seven brides for seven emperors, and here is the eighth and
there is the ninth, peeking like a dark dawn over sandstone
Hills where we will not talk of how we spent summer nights
as children, dewed and cool as ice cream, enlivened as protest
song – a lolly stick and a lathi are both made from wood but

let us talk of nothing that reminds us of the Jamun. Tell me
instead how many times you can say the word beloved.
Back when the bijli went for hours
in our homes across the great eighth city
we would gather like moths to the tungsten. Someone was
always playing Krishna's flute. Pinwheels framed the stars.
Where now do we go for light-ness? But let us not write now of
erosions, of the many baghs we should have watered and
kept safe. It is late, come, let us let the old Jamuns sleep.

Enter

I find the rituals of religion,
their stories and secrets,
so beautiful.
Like small doorways
to the divine.

Who was the first person to say –

The doorways to my home
are better than yours.
More beautiful and ornate,
larger, more intricate.

And how come they didn't say instead –

Come friend.
You take your doorway
and I will take mine.
I cannot wait to see you on the other side.
We will meet in the same place,
in the courtyard with the unending sky,
in the lap of the divine,
and discuss our journeys
over a shared cup of wine.

Pray for the World or the One That Spawned the Hashtag (2015)

It is not Paris we should pray for.
It is the world.
It is a world in which Beirut,
reeling from bombings two days before Paris,
is not covered in the press.
A world in which a bomb goes off
at a funeral in Baghdad
and not one person's 'status update' says 'Baghdad'
because not one white person died in that fire.
Pray for the world
that blames a refugee crisis for a terrorist attack.
That does not pause to differentiate between the attacker
and the person running from the very same thing you are.
Pray for a world
where people walking across countries for months,
their only belongings upon their backs,
are told they have no place to go.
Say a prayer for Paris by all means,
but pray more
for a world that does not have a prayer
for those who no longer have a home to defend.
For a world that is falling apart in all corners,
and not simply in the towers and cafes we find so familiar.

2020

The word of the year is somehow not *helpless*,
I hear – how can that be after the tragedy we've built,
an entire colosseum of pain. Museums of defiance
in coffees and marble cakes and online posts that already
feel dated in the meekness of their suffering.
I asked my grandmother who remembers
the Americans entering her village, her neighbours
burying the book, if it is worse now. She confirms
what I thought, says she never before feared losing
a planet; a country was as bad as it got back then in the
jolly days of carpet bombings and what-not. Favourite
old films hollow in their rampant happiness. On screen
couples meet at a concert, a party, a bar. *Just like that?*
And on worse days – *What is a concert?* On a good evening
I hear myself lament like an old lady – Oh! For simpler times.
My heart despairs for all the young girls who will not get
to kiss sweet strangers. Everyone is erudite. They *know*.
All I know is my body is foolish, first thing she walks out
the door she'll be stepping into illness so I stay put and
do sit-ups with unnecessary fervour. Who will see this
stomach so taut? Who even cares? So I watch the news,
a manic list of humans dying,
leaving the world in thousands –
the soul factory is full, a rave of batty humans has arrived.
No one wants to talk about the poor walking home or

climate change, that thing as far away as a village.
Look, the shoulders of the Earth are stooped.
She knows when the next war comes,
they'll dunk her head in water,
hold her down till it fills her lungs
and her skin goes all blue.
Till her extremities are cold,
and lifeless.

Hope.

It is desire dressed in humility,

and a wish, whispering a saint's name.

It is want, when want is nobility,

and madness, when madness is sane.

VII

You and me and all
the strawberries know: summer
comes then spring must go.

Tomorrow

We were not made for this world
you with your love of the stars,
me with my compassion
for the changing moods of clouds.
We should move to a cottage on a hill somewhere,
grow tomatoes, sow stories, watch two-toned dahlias
come up around us for air.
We should sleep nights by a river,
or even the sea,
argue over whether water sounds more like bells or cymbals.
I want to worry over your insect bites,
adopt stray mountain dogs,
sassy ginger seaside cats,
and cultivate comical chickens
we later won't have the heart to eat.
We weren't made for this,
these tall cities of mainly smoke.
We were made for orange trees and summer breeze
lives so free
we forget the weary weight of our feet
and give our bodies over
to life's extraordinary stream.

'Mummy, mummy what is this thing "breeze"?'

'Oh don't bother with that honey, it's just the gossip of leaves.'

// 21st-Century Parenting and Why the World May End

Indian Summer

And just like that
in a flurry of white cotton
and rustling green leaves,
rarest blue skies
and skirts above the knee,
blankets from Jaipur
and anklets from Kutch,
flame of the Forest
and ruby sherbet…
Summer arrived.
Just like that.

Monsoon III

If there's a word for 'lover of rain'
replace it forever
from now
with my name.

Monsoon IV

You have rain outside and a window to watch it through.
You have no business not being in love with the world.

Monsoon V

Eleven looks like seven
we wake late, damp cluster
kindred to soil to raindrops.
I remember your body is
seventy percent water and
I am thirsting but first there are
spotted doves growling in the window box
expertly mimicking thunder breath above
the dousing of gulmohar fire.
Rain the oldest miracle in the world
has arrived to turn the neem tree neon.
Flowers like gemstones emerge,
there is the skirted mystery of fungi
each morning furring the underside
of every log we hunt out and we say it like this –
FUN GUY! like children, shouting delight, unscared.
This allowance for silliness, for parakeet pantomime
for soaked shirts somehow (now that we have survived school)
not indecent, feels like time latched.
The gift of free water.
When a guest comes to your home,
the scripture says – you may not refuse them water.
Here we are, heady and transparent
on this small spinning planet
that is reminding us
we do not belong.

Folk Song II

We could have been so many things
You and I.
We could have been doctors in East Africa,
or teachers in the Pyrenees,
we could have sailed blue boats to unseen isles,
or fed mandarins to chimpanzees.
We could have built a ship that went to space,
collected honey off wild mango trees,
learnt a thousand languages,
you Spanish, me Polish,
and maybe together Cantonese.
We could have moved to Budapest,
discovered hidden treasure chests,
spent our lives on the South China Sea,
spent our lives in ecstasy!
We could have had children,
made money by the million,
given it all up to start anew.
We could have been so many things,
alas my darling,
I and you.

VIII

Even in the wake
of all this ache … I continue.
I must continue.

Greener

My entire childhood is contained in
the staccato hills of the stegosaurus back.
Over time I discarded things like
the desire for a tongue piercing, boyfriends and violet hair,
but the first memories of tasting a Jamun
(same colour after all)
still do things to my mouth no metal ring could dream of.
In the early days things like
a ladybird on a single blade of grass
next to a forget-me-not field (two feet by six feet)
behind my neighbour's house
on a huge six-foot high mountain, mattered.
You should have seen that mountain
we summited it once every seven minutes
move over Tenzing.
We would roll down it, the journey lasting and lasting,
then lie in the foothills, breathless, heads a-spin with giggles
before re-beginning the long-legged climb.
My dog was a wolf in those days.
Today he is smoke.
We sucked popsicles made of radioactive particles.
Do you remember the shiver of first finding that green?
Do you remember learning the word Chlorophyll?
Say it – klo-ro-fill.
Do you remember the taste in your mouth
the first time the skin of your knee came exposed

on the gravelly back road, peeling back, caving in,
blood seeping through the white dust of your dry skin?
Do you remember the metal smell drift about your nostrils,
and the terror of iodine-soaked cotton.

Then vast years followed, where all this ceased to matter.
I began to care about bigger things.
For a while in the middle I thought
ladybirds had gone extinct.
I want to elevate everyday like every day was
when I was 4
and 6 and 9.

So I am learning how to fall once more
to bruise my knees and scrape flesh
from palms grown too close to keys.
Tumbling into teacups
falling for the loop of their handles
and the sexy curve of their lips.
I want to explain to you
the transparency of a teabag.
I want to make a dress of it
wear it to the teddy bear's picnic.
The perfection of the sharpened colour pencil
has come back to me all these years later.
The leaf left as bookmark inside some book.

I wake and appreciate that at 8 o'clock
the light falls on my bed so that it slices it
exactly in half and for a short while,
with nothing but a roll of my hips,
I can choose to sleep in a sunny day
or a cool evening – what magic is this?

My dog is still smoke today but I can summon him as I wish.
I love how the fishbones line up in parallel spikes
like a rake in the flowerbeds of my china plate
(maybe those are forget-me-nots, look at that shade of blue).
I love how my lover's stubble rises to my fingertips.
The ants building a highway across my kitchen floor.
The hyped hour before sunset when the world
is washed with sad gold.
I love the way my doorbell rings twice when you come home.
I love the soft underside of my own arm.
I love the soft underside of my own heart
where the long veins of memory are made
I dig there with a brutally soft spade.

Be brave
be kind
live gently
but with fire.

Who Am I But a Vessel for Wonder?

So much happens for you to push the muscled doors of your plush heart closed. For you to shut it up and away, make it small, tucked into the bounty of your flesh, safe against the swift rushes of pain you know now intimately. People you care for as your own will die, have died, sometimes suddenly, often too early and without notice, without any signs of illness or disease, like a trick. Terribly, terribly sometimes by their own hand or in the drastic unfurling of fate and you have shook your head and muttered untruths about how only angels go early. Businesses you nurture like plants will fold (the plants won't last either), those we adore will run off with lovers who are more beautiful and sometimes you'll hear about children murdering parents, sometimes the other way round like such a thing were even possible. What is possible and not will capsize and then come up for air transformed many times over in your lifetime. What is possible will be drowned. Oceans then moons were once breached, planets tomorrow. At the same time here on a humbled neglected Earth coups and wars will continue and ordinary people suffer the shame of those who have no time to feel it. We will not escape the news, the breaking guilt of it and of knowing that just to be alive is grace. Cancer will come and we will not always be able to fight it. It will erode the bodies of those we love and us, sitting silent within skin like the devil, waiting. Perhaps most devastatingly, pets will leave us, small paws clicking off to some other place. There is still no way to avoid the common cold, and books will be borrowed and not returned – sprouting a different sort of hate. But you must keep your heart open. You must keep it big and growing, flexing its muscles constantly like lungs for air, like wingspan. Do not hurt because you have been hurt. Do not close your heart like a house in disuse, to protect it. Against all odds (and there are many) you must notice the basic, first facts. The shape of the clouds, the myriad colours of flowers, the smell of fresh coffee and the stars on a glistening winter night. You cannot forego the mystic wonder of aeroplanes and physics, baby animals of every species and the childhood dreams of dinosaurs. The silly delight of rain, home, running, even of two people thinking the exact same thing at the exact same time and calling it special. The thrill of chasing a butterfly in a shade of blue your eyes have never witnessed before. And how now it is part of the language of your imagination. To keep your eyes witnessing, caressing a world as it perhaps collapses. The rousting satisfaction of catching a ball – the sound it makes as it socks to your palm. The miracle of walking of music of fire and food. No matter how rich or poor you grow, to never lose the yelping joy of finding a coin in the street, or what melody can do for a soul. I do not know what works for you, or if there is a manual for granting mercy to the self, but this is what works for me – to approach the world with wonder. With the simplicity of kindness, assumption of the best intent always, curious days, gentle nights and to keep my heart open, muscles pushed wide, against all odds.

Things to Keep

a lock of your lover's hair
your word
good wine in the kitchen cupboard just in case
quiet
a box in your bedroom (to collect the clothes you
intend to give to charity)
trying
water in bowls on the balcony, for the birds
flowers pressed into the pages of books
your mother's old saris
this poem
going
some love in your heart

Gathering

It is time to gather the pieces of my heart
I scattered
like white pigeons
each hoping to bring you home.
It's time to call in
the armies of my heart,
it's time for them
to tend to their own.

Self-care is birds, I think.
Self-care is seeing them spread out,
bereft of nausea, swirling, bereft
of drugs of any kind of high
but joy in the long routine of centuries.
Self-care is hearing and admitting
and saying my heart is a bird
my heart is pieces of white pigeon
my heart is no hunter
no adventure seeker
no hawk
my heart is fluffy and look, alone and –
nesting.

Joy

I had forgotten how to have fun with my words
because I was writing them for other people –
– people who wanted such serious things!
But me? I want some wine,
world peace,
crocodiles to keep their skin,
elephants their teeth,
many baked goods on Sunday
and countries to loosen their borders.
Now if that doesn't strike you as joyous,
my friend, what will?

I see now
my aching heart had no place
in this universe's grand plans.
In a world where the swift rising sea still
points the even side of its enormous finger
to its sister, the punctual swelling sodium moon
to show the whale, breathtaker, which way to go.
In a world where fast disappearing birds
still swim valiantly the sky in patterns,
stitching with wind-thread, star to star,
masters of their cosmic shibori.
Where flowers fertilized by blood might sprout
from between walls in houses
in the shattered midst of other people's wars
so a child may finally know colour and nectar
and yes, poetry.
My tawdry aching heart
had no place amidst
that which seeks
miracle.

Go. Now chase what is wild.
And I will bring you home
every single time.

Notes

The poem 'Submission' was inspired by Italo Calvino's book *Invisible Cities*, a fictional account of places visited by Marco Polo and relayed to Kublai Khan. The phrase 'lost sparrows of Delhi' refers to the dwindling numbers of the little bird. In 2012, mostly due to urbanization, their original population was said to have dropped by up to 70 per cent. The sparrow was adopted as the 'state bird' of Delhi, in an attempt to raise awareness, but a decade later it is uncertain as to whether there has been any improvement.

The poem 'A Personal Manual to Make a Heart Stop Hurting' was written for a friend. In 2016, I was always busy, or maybe pretending to be. In the midst of that crowded life I received a message. It said – 'What is the best way to make a heart stop hurting?' The poem was written as response. The day after I published it, a girl from North Carolina wrote to me saying – 'One of my favourite musicals came through my state and I wanted to go but my ex and I split a few months ago, and I am still struggling with being alone. Tonight was the last showing, and an hour before it started, I bought the very last single-seat ticket they had, and took myself to the show.'

The poem 'Heroine' was first written for the lovely people of Studio Renn in 2019.

'Write About What Hurts' was written in response to the Indian government's plans for the Central Vista project, which will see the demolishment of the National Museum and the Annexe to the National Archives of India, the latter a historical treasure trove of 45 lakh files including 25,000 rare manuscripts, more than 1 lakh Mughal documents, 1 lakh maps and 6 lakh post-Partition era documents.[1] Worryingly, the government remains vague on the subject of the storage of the priceless material contained within both buildings. The museum contains Buddhist relics and the famed Harappan dancing girl.[2] The project will also see the demolition of the Indira Gandhi National Centre for the Arts which was launched in 1985 at a ceremony where five rocks from five Indian rivers – Indus, Ganga, Kaveri, Mahanadi and Narmada – were brought to Delhi. The foundation stone was laid within an ancient Deodar tree and then five other trees – the Sacred Fig or Bodhi, the Banyan, the Ashoka, the Arjuna and the Kadamba[3] – were planted at the site which will no longer exist, making way instead for ten new office buildings.[4] Most heartbreakingly,

---

1 https://scroll.in/article/999629/indias-national-archives-might-go-partly-out-of-reach-for-writers-what-happens-to-their-holdings

2 https://www.ndtv.com/india-news/delhis-3-iconic-buildings-national-museum-indira-gandhi-national-centre-for-the-arts-national-archives-annexe-set-to-be-demolished-for-central-vista-p-2443645

3 http://ignca.gov.in/about-ignca/inauguration/

4 https://www.thehindu.com/news/national/ignca-to-be-demolished-relocated-as-part-of-central-vista-revamp/article30573196.ece

Central Vista will most likely see the felling of an avenue's worth of century-old Jamun trees. An old prophecy about the seven cities of Delhi, that's been oft-quoted in this time goes – 'Whoever builds a new city in Delhi, will lose it.'[5] Ironically, this poem was completed the day a different government 'refurbishment' was inaugurated – the new Jallianwala Bagh Memorial.

Personal notes on the poem 'Pray for the World':

In November 2015, a series of coordinated terrorist attacks took place in the city of Paris. In the hours that followed, I wrote a poem and posted it on the internet. By midnight the poem has been shared one hundred thousand times and the poem's title 'Pray for the World' and corresponding hashtag were trending globally. By the end of the week the numbers were in the millions. When I had uploaded the poem, I hadn't added my name so the wider audience did not know I'd written it. It had travelled so fast across the globe, I hadn't had the time to catch up. Newspapers across the world shared it, actors and musicians shared it, and then Paulo Coelho shared it on Twitter to ten million followers, after 'correcting' the lines he found 'offensive', and without crediting the original poet.[6] While there is a greater conversation about art, ownership, anonymity and virality here, there is also simply

---

5 William Dalrymple quoting Iris Portal speaking the old prophecy in *City of Djinns*.

6 He deleted the tweet some days later.

the question of voicelessness. Those who wish to find you, can and will. I found this out in the many heartbreaking letters of appreciation and solidarity I received from around the world and in the professionalism of those like the BBC, who traced the poem to Delhi and then me. I also found it out in the death threats and hate mail that came from those tracking me for different reasons. It was an extraordinary time and a part of me did not want to include the poem in this collection. Relevant as the themes may still sadly be, I feel its time has passed, and there are many who have echoed this sentiment far better than I, in the years between then and now. I relented finally because this poem began within me the complex internal journey of accepting myself as a poet, of growing comfortable with hearing people call me one. More crucially, it showed me for the first time the twisted magic and ultimate power of what a poem can do.

'Greener' was first written for wonderful Anahita Kayan of The Space at 9/2 in 2017. The phrase 'brutally soft' used in the closing lines of the poem is from the poet Nayyirah Waheed's book *Salt*.

Acknowledgements

My editor Swati Daftuar, who believed a few squares on social media could become a book, who put her heart into making it happen, and who waited out the worst of a pandemic. Thank you for all this but also for taking my emojis in stride. Gratitude to you, Ananth Padmanabhan, Diya Kar, Bonita Shimray, Shabnam Srivastava, and the team at HarperCollins India for patience and persistence and for giving poetry space.

Cheer-givers, in this hard time in particular: Diya Katyal, Neha Kaul Mehra, Eina Ahluwalia, Sulagna Ghosh, Mihika Tewari, Radhika Burman, Anjum Katyal, Shabba Hakim, Anand Puri, Munir Mohanty.

Rewant Lokesh – thank you for rescuing me technologically, two books in a row.

Special thanks to Saba Azad for steadying thoughts on anxiety and the artistic process, and for so, so much else in the final days of editing. Puja Amin, for being a pillar for my poetry, from its very foundations. Anirudh Nair, you make me a better artist and also a better person – our conversations carry me through the years. Thank you for eyes, ears, recitations. David Earp you are Krishna, beloved of a thousand ladies, of song, and butter. You give so much of yourself. It felt like you were by my side this entire while, not continents away. Thank you for your magic. Mridula Pai, for the Eliot incantation that graces the start of this book, for early essential edits, for your shoulder on some really difficult days. Aanchal Malhotra for every moment of sharing laughter, literature, grief and learning.

Sharanya Manivannan, for fierceness, for gentleness, for swift praise.

Ratna Pathak Shah, I don't believe they make humans with your grace any longer. I will always be sincerely thankful for your depth of heart and your prophecies.

Sampurna Chattarji, seamstress, mentor, Space Gulliver. Such immense gratitude for your confidence and kindness, but also for secret affinities and kinship, unexpected and joyous. And for making the editing of this book a multi-sensory experience, and a lesson in generosity.

Rhea Gupte, I want to thank you for this unfaultable cover, your art, the dual gift of your soulfulness and intellect, but also for reminding me about choices. You are my compass for where beauty exists. Thank you for the wonder of you.

Shruti Debi, here's to laughing through it all. Thank you for breaking it down when I break down. I want other writers to heed this – if you're not discussing shampoos with your agent, be very suspicious.

To everyone on my Instagram who has asked for years – 'Where is the poetry book?' Here it is. Thank you for waiting.

My parents – Kalpana Misra and Rajen Parikh.

My sisters – Nayantara and Danika Parikh.

My love – Amitesh Prosad Ray.

Thank you.